The Thing That Lived Upstairs

A True Story of a Frightful Childhood Event

By LaVone C. Hicks

Library of Congress Control Number: 2015901676
Publisher: Hicks & Assoc., Goldsboro, NC

ISBN:
ISBN-13:978-0-9861175-0-

ISBN:
ISBN-13:978-0-9861175-0-

DEDICATION

This book is dedicated to the students of Carver Elementary School in Mt. Olive, NC; my grandchildren Gregory, Kelis, and Dariyus; my sister, Patricia C. Ford; my mother, the late Jessie McKinnon Coley; and to all who are challenged to face their fears.

ACKNOWLEDGEMENTS

Were it not for the grace of God I would never have had the mindset or ability to write anything. To God be all the glory!

Preface

Fear can be a powerful thing. Yet there is the kind of fear that some people crave like that of riding a tall, winding, rollercoaster. Why would anyone want to ride it again? Just for the sheer excitement of course.

Then there's the kind of fear that causes the heart to beat ferociously due to the possibility of being harmed by the unknown. This kind of fear can almost cause one to faint. This fear is the kind that little Vone experienced in this true story. As we proceed, let us set the atmosphere in which this story takes place.

It happened in the late 1950's when she was around five years old that Vone had the scariest experience of her youth. The setting was in a two-story wooden house on a tree-lined street in a small town of eastern North Carolina. She lived there with her mother, grandmother, and older sister Pat. Though the house that they rented had six bedrooms, they did not use the three bedrooms upstairs. So the landlord kept those rooms under lock and key.

She and her sister shared a bed in the same downstairs bedroom with their mother who had a separate bed of her own. This was fine with Vone since she was so timid, the very opposite of her confident sister. Her mom's and sister's presence offered the security she needed at the time. Plus this arrangement gave her someone to snuggle up to for warmth in the cold winter.

She used to like the jittery feeling it gave her to go upstairs with Pat and peek through the keyhole of a locked bedroom. She could smell the dust and see silhouettes of covered furniture in the dim light emitted by the evening sun. Her sister would tap her on the shoulder unexpectedly and say, "It's a man sitting on a chair!" as she dashed away, leaving Vone screaming at the top of the stairs.

At the bottom of the stairs was a wooden door to the right that had a square hole cut at the bottom of the side that opened into the den. *(Perhaps the former tenants had a pet that used it to go in and out.)* To the right of the den was the kitchen, and to the left was their back bedroom. Big Ma, as they affectionately called her grandma, had a room right of the kitchen and in the front of the house.

Robert Hall 2015©

Her nightmare began one night when everyone had drifted off to sleep except her. It was hard to keep her eyes off the spooky shadows cast on the walls by the kerosene lamp that was used for a night light. So it didn't help at all when she heard a noise coming from the room above her. Then it moved to the top of the stairs. Her hair felt like it stood on its ends when the mysterious thing began to descend slowly with a "kathump, kathump, kathump". "Maybe it's a mouse", she told herself. But the footsteps were too heavy for a mouse. She hated to wake her mama who worked so hard every day at a cleaners pressing clothes. When she'd hit the bed she'd be out like a light. The perpetrator went through the hole in the door and to the right into the kitchen, "ch-ch-ch", and began pillaging through the cardboard box that was used for garbage. She had no choice. Vone said fearfully, "Mama, do you hear that?" Mama continued to snore. It moved to the china cabinet where they kept pots and pans in the bottom and plates and glasses near the top. The pans began to rattle and the dishes clattered. She trembled with fear from the tip of her toes to the ends of her long braided plaits. She whined, louder this time, "Mama, do you hear that?" Her mama said sleepily, "Yea, baby I hear it. But just go to sleep. It'll be alright." Vone gave a deep sigh of disappointment. Her eyes were wide open as she strained to hear its next move. After a while, when it was done exploring, it returned through the hole and up the stairs, "kathump, kathump, kathump", it sounded. Back into the room above her it went and nestled down right above her head. The tired little girl finally drifted off to sleep.

Well, Vone got up the next day and went to school, which she loved to do. She forgot all about what had happened the night before. As she stepped off the school bus at the end of the day and skipped towards her front door, she was overwhelmed with the delicious aroma of Big Ma's freshly baked homemade biscuits coming from the kitchen and through the screen door. She loved to "sop" molasses or eat some of Big Ma's homemade apple jelly or pear preserves with her biscuits. She finished dinner, did her homework, and went out to play. Later, as she prepared for bed, Pat poured hot water into a large metal tub. It had heated from the kettle that had been on the wood-burning stove in the den. They cooled the boiling water with cold water and took their baths in the tub.

It was not until Vone jumped into bed and was nearly asleep that the noise above her reminded her of the circumstances from the night before. "Oh no!," she thought. "It wasn't a dream after all." The same scenario happened just as it did the night before. The rambling noises continued as her privacy and sleep were once more invaded. Her mama was no help because she was so tired. Vone wished so hard that her mom and dad would marry, then he'd be there to take care of this situation. But this frightening activity went on night after night.

Finally her prayers for a resolution to the night prowler problem were answered due to an unusual situation. You see, one night as her mom was changing the linens on her bed, a yellowish liquid began to drip from the leaky ceiling and onto her clean white sheets, and it wasn't even raining outside! Vone had never seen her mama get so mad. Her mama exclaimed, "Oh no you won't. There's no way I'm gonna let anything **pee** on my bed! Tonight when it comes down I'm going into that kitchen and I'm not coming out until I find out what it is!" Vone thought, "Yaaaay."

Robert Hall '2015©

So her mama armed herself with the metal poker that was used to stir the coals in the pot-bellied wood-burning stove. She sat at the foot of the bed and waited with determination in her eyes. She was set like a race horse waiting for the signal. Sure enough, when it was quiet and dark outside, there came the familiar sound down the steps,"kathump, kathump, kathump." Through the hole in the door and into the kitchen it went, "ch-ch-ch." Her mama stood up and looked them in the eye. "Alright young'uns. Now I'm going to see what this is," she said. "Don't you be scared. I'm gonna close the door behind me." Her mama marched out of the bedroom, pulling the door tightly behind her. Off she stalked like a hunter going on a safari. Vone kept her head under the covers as she listened intently. At first she heard nothing. It was so quiet until she could literally hear her heart pounding. Then suddenly a tremendous noise was heard from the kitchen." Bamalam-a-lam-a lam." Vone froze, not knowing what was happening.

Soon all was quiet again. Pat and Vone were peeking from underneath the covers with anticipation. They saw the ivory colored door knob slowly turning. The door began to open gradually with a "creeeeak". They were shivering as they held onto each other for dear life when they heard their mother's voice. "Wanna see what it is?" she said eerily. With mixed emotions as their big brown eyes peeked just over the heavy patchwork quilt, they nodded their heads up and down in a positive agreement. Their mama brought it out from behind her slowly as she held it by the tail. To their surprise it was an ……………….

Opossum! It seemed to be smiling. Their mom proceeded to tell them what happened. She stated that it kept slipping out of her reach as she struck at it underneath the table. But when she cornered it between the china cabinet and the refrigerator it just stood still and grinned. Then she knocked it out with the metal pole. Later, she gave it to their next door neighbor who made himself a delightful 'possum stew. *(Back then, people ate small, wild animals such as squirrels, birds, rabbits, and opossum.)*

Robert Hall '2015©

So this ended the saga of the thing that lived upstairs. As she grew older, Vone reluctantly had to move out of her mama's room and right into that very room upstairs where the opossum had resided. She soon overcame her fear and slept many peaceful nights in the room upstairs. Maybe ol' 'possum has a sister or brother **in your house!**

The End!

An opossum looks like a giant gray rat. He is a scavenger and eats almost anything. These marsupials nurse their young and carry them on their back or in a pouch like kangaroos. Like bats, they come out at night and can hang upside down from a limb by their tails. When threatened by predators, they play dead. Thus the term "playing 'possum" was formed when someone pretends to be asleep.

Glossary

Anticipation- expectation or prediction

Descend- move or fall downward

Determination- firmness of purpose

Emitted- produced or discharged

Invaded- occupied or entered

Linens- fabric household goods such as bedding

Literally- actually was

Overwhelmed- to surge over; engulf

Plait- a single length of hair made up of three or more interlaced strands

Pot-bellied- having a large, round stomach that sticks out

Prowler- a person who goes stealthily about with some unlawful intentions, as to commit a burglary or theft.

Reluctantly- feeling or showing doubt about doing something

Resolution- the act of finding an answer or solution to a conflict or problem.

Safari- a journey or expedition, for hunting, exploration, or investigation.

Saga- a long, involved story, account, or series of incidents.

Scenario- a description of what could possibly happen

Silhouette- the image of a person, animal, object, or scene represented as a solid shape...

Sop- a piece of bread soaked in a liquid

Tenants- people who occupy land or property rented from a landlord.

Timid- showing a lack of courage or confidence; easily frightened

Definitions taken from Merriam-Webster Online, Wikipedia-the free encyclopedia, Dictionary reference.com

About The Author

So how does a music teacher of thirty-four years become the author of two books in less than six months? Maybe it was in LaVone Hicks' DNA, since her grandfather who she hardly knew, James R. Walker Sr, wrote several books of poetry. But she believes it was all divinely orchestrated, starting with her earning a BA in music from Johnson C. Smith University in Charlotte, NC in 1976. The stage was set when she added a master's degree in education with a concentration in reading from UNC-Charlotte, NC. In retrospect, it was no coincidence that her master's thesis was entitled, *How to Teach Reading through Music.*

In the early 2000's, she reluctantly taught Guided Reading before her music classes began each day, which was required by her school district of all special area teachers. Little did she know that it was an essential part of God's plan. As she also developed her skills as an entrepreneur over the last nineteen years in insurance, she became keenly aware of how little she and many educators knew about money. So in August of 2014 she published her first book, *Who Wants to Be a Millionaire-Life Lessons Learned.*

It was her students at Carver Elementary School in Mt. Olive NC, however, who inspired her to publish again so soon. Though born in Goldsboro NC, she has been telling them the true story of the thing that frightened her in her childhood when she lived in Fremont NC every year since 2003. She had forgotten that she had even prepared her story for a Guided Reading lesson years ago.

It is her hope that *The Thing That Lived Upstairs* will not only entertain for years to come, but will also educate others about life in the 1950's and be a legacy to her elementary school, her friends, and her family.